Dedicated to my friend George Stahnke who came looking for me at Horesh. May his tribe increase.

"Jonathan went to David at Horesh and helped him find strength in God."
1 Samuel 23:16

Isolation in Ministry
© 2019 Gene M. Roncone II

Table of Contents

Introduction

I feel the ground moving beneath me! Like shifting tectonic plates, something is changing in the church and it's not good. Pastors are leaving the ministry, taking their own lives and suffering from depression in record numbers. Author Richard Clinton claims that 70% of those who enter the ministry will not retire from it.[1] We are experiencing a national crisis among our ministers that can't be ignored.

It's not until you dig down beneath the symptoms of burn out, loneliness and moral failure that you begin to see the real problem...isolation. For various reasons, ministers have allowed themselves to become separated from life-giving relationships, empathetic peers and healthy accountability.

This e-book examines the cause, consequences and cure for isolation in ministry. It is the product of a five-part PODumentary that I syndicated in 2019 on THE COMMUNITY podcast.[2] I spent months researching this multifaceted issue and all the latest research and best thinking pointed to one undeniable fact. **We need each other.** But, that should not surprise us. The Bible has proclaimed that for centuries saying,

> *"Do not give up meeting together, as some are in the habit of doing, but encouraging one another—and all the more as you see the Day approaching." (Hebrews 10:25 NIV)*

God's Word is not only saying that we need each other, but also claiming that we will need each other more and more the closer we get to the Second Coming of Christ. That is why this e-book has been created as a tool to spur more discussion, collaboration and brainstorming by ministers and denominational leaders alike. After all, we really are...

Better together,

Gene Roncone

Chapter 1

Is Isolation in Ministry Real?

Over the past few years I've noticed a pattern that is ruining lives, paralyzing churches and resulting in tragic loss. I have lost three ministerial colleagues to suicide. When you dig through the ashes of depression, moral failure, anxiety and burnout there seems to be one thing at the bottom—isolation. I call it the *Archipelago Effect*.

An archipelago is a collection of small islands separated by water. By this, I mean that as our own personal and local ministry needs have become more diverse, we have drifted further and further from each other. Instead of being a tightknit community with definite boundaries, we have become a nation of microscopic islands. For example, instead of being a large land mass unified by diversity, we have become more like Micronesia (a nation with hundreds of isolated islands).

I don't believe this phenomenon is unique to just my area. It's occurring nearly everywhere and just now coming on radar. While we ministers are preaching and teaching about the importance of small groups and community, most of us are living in isolation. Many reputable research groups seem to agree.

- A recent study by LifeWay Research found nearly one in four pastors acknowledge they have personally struggled with depression or anxiety.[3]
- Chuck Hannaford, a clinical psychologist who consults for the Southern Baptist Convention, said he believes the

rate of pastoral suicides has increased during his 30 years of practice and he expects the number will continue to rise.[4]

- In his book, *How to Ruin Your Life*, Eric Geiger named isolation as one of the most common causes of personal implosion.[5]
- Barna Research's 2017 report on "The State of Pastors" reported that only one-third of ministers expressed a high level of satisfaction with their personal friendships. Around one in three said they were dissatisfied with their relationships.[6]
- Another study reported similar findings. After surveying 1,000 protestant pastors, they found over half of the pastors (55%) agree it is easy to get discouraged in ministry. The majority of pastors agree that ministry makes them feel lonely. Regarding friendships, 64% of pastors have five or fewer close friends within their church, and 26% have less than two.[7]

In order to get practical feedback on the subject, I sought out two professional counselors, George Stahnke and Susan Schmidt, with knowledge on the effects of isolation. Stahnke[8] has been in ministry for 40 years, is a full-time counselor at Focus on the Family and the founder of Renewal Ministries in Colorado Springs. The Southern Baptist Convention subcontracts their pastoral emergency calls to Focus on the Family, and Stahnke is part of the team that picks up those calls. So, when it comes to knowledge about ministers in crisis, he is on the front lines.

Schmidt[9] is a licensed professional counselor from Roseville, California. She has over thirty years ministry experience both as an ordained minister and a minister's wife. She has been in private practice for twenty-three years. Having grown up in the church as the daughter of a denominational executive, many of Susan's clients come from a ministry background. Many are either ministers or ministers' spouses.

When asked about how serious of a threat isolation in ministry is today, Stahnke believes the hardest part is not having others to turn to who understand the challenges and stress that go along with the role. As a result, ministry leaders are forced to rely on their own spiritual and emotional strength, which can wear thin over time. This contributes to the leader feeling anger, despair, disappointment and hopelessness, with nobody to help shoulder the burden. Schmidt adds that isolation not only affects the ministry leader, but can take a major toll on the spouse as well. As his/her partner puts so much time and energy into ministry, the spouse may develop feelings of loneliness and seclusion, which can lead to depression.

Throughout this book, we'll address the topics that surround the issue of isolation in ministry. It's our hope that straightforward communication about this topic will expose this dangerous threat and help many of us rebuild a deeper commitment to community.

MAKING IT REAL: Questions for personal reflection or group discussion.

1. The introduction spoke of pastors leaving the ministry, taking their own lives and suffering from depression in record numbers. How have you seen signs of this in your own local context?
2. When speaking of the lack of community between local churches and ministers, Gene said, "Instead of being a tightknit community with definite boundaries, we have become a nation of microscopic islands." Do you agree with this observation? Why or why not?
3. Why do you think ministers preach and teach about the need for community but lack it in their own lives and ministry?
4. Have you seen isolation negatively effect spouses in ministry? If so, how?
5. What indicators do you see in your spouse that may indicate he or she may be leaning into loneliness and isolation? (both spouses answer)
6. Do you feel that your loneliness is in any way connected to the real demands made on you as a minister?

7. When you experience loneliness, would you say it is in response to a triggering event, or more of a backpack that you carry around routinely?

Chapter 2

Lonely Losers: The Cost of Isolation

Now that we have established how pervasive the problem is, we need to bring to light the high price people pay for remaining isolated. There are many costs of isolation, but I have identified five that specifically pertain to ministry.

1. **Isolated leaders are more susceptible to temptation.** There is one thing I have learned...ministry will find your weakness! Whatever your weakness is, the enemy will try to capitalize on it and that usually starts with some form of isolation. Dietrich Bonhoeffer once said, "Sin demands to have a man by himself. We must resist the temptation to live and serve in isolation. For the sake of our own souls."[10]

   When probed about the connection between isolation and temptation, Schmidt points out that Jesus taught us about this connection in scripture. In Luke's gospel, we see Jesus specifically warning the disciples that "Satan desires to sift you" (Luke 22:31). The purpose of a sifter is to separate, or to single something out, from the rest of the flour. Since we are meant for meaningful connection, being deprived of it weakens us. It can cause a lack of resilience and we start to feel unfortified inside, thus making us more vulnerable to temptation. Isolated leaders will have a greater challenge resisting temptation, since they aren't experiencing the warmth and strength of the fortifying connections for which God wired them.

Stahnke reminds us that *everyone* is tempted on a daily basis. There are no exceptions. Isolation increases the risk of acting upon our temptations because there is no one to help us cope, recover, nor keep us accountable.

2. **Isolated leaders become dangerous leaders.** Eric Geiger said, "The sting of criticism, the burden of the responsibilities and the pace of leadership can nudge a leader toward isolation, but every step toward isolation is a step toward danger."[11]

Isolated leaders lack meaningful relationships that are not connected to their work or supervision structures. They separate themselves from support systems, accountability structures and peer communication. Care and encouragement from others can be hard to come by. With no authentic accountability system, despite all their gifts and strengths, their weaknesses can win over. We are reminded of the dangers of this in Proverbs 15:22, *"Plans fail for lack of counsel, but with many advisers they succeed."*

3. **Isolated leaders are more prone to destructive emotions.** It's a statistical fact that isolated leaders experience more frequent and intense feelings of sadness, loneliness, depression, anxiety and stress.

In September of 2018, we were all shocked to learn of the suicide of mega church pastor, Andrew Stoecklein. At the age of 30, Andrew Stoecklein seemingly had it all—a thriving ministry, a wonderful wife, three beautiful boys and some of the finest parents and mentors a young minister could hope to have. Stoecklein himself, about a week before his suicide, said, "My church was thriving, growing and moving, but I was crumbling, exhausted, weak and tired." Sadly, Andrew Stoecklein had everything but the desire to live.

In an interview with Barna Research, family therapist and former pastor, Jim Hawkins, says that a minister's close and authentic relationships can be both a preventive medicine and an antidote for emotional wounds, mental illness, depression and even some addictions.[12]

When questioned about why isolation can take us to such a dark emotional place, and asked to share some of the destructive emotions that isolation has brought about in their clients, Stahnke and Schmidt both mention the lack of emotional support driving their clients into states of depression and anxiety. Stahnke points out that although ministry can be fulfilling and exciting, there is another side that can be stressful, disappointing and heartbreaking. When we go through times of stress alone, without the needed emotional support, there can be a significant increase in anxiety and depression that negatively affects our ability to cope. We continue to ponder and reflect on negative experiences, mentally and verbally demeaning ourselves or others. This can lead to self-medication with pornography, drugs, alcohol or gambling.

Schmidt feels that isolation cuts us off from the "nutrients" our mental health needs that can only be supplied by human connection. When it comes to mental health, no one does better in solitude. Research continues to reconfirm the fact that no one thrives alone. God simply did not create us to operate this way. We need to realize the significance of the fact that even *before* the fall, God told Adam that it was not good for him to be alone. What Schmidt frequently sees in her practice are ministry wives beginning to experience increased anxiety, fear, discouragement, and feelings of being invisible and insignificant. When these kinds of feelings are kept inside, they grow, often to a level of clinical depression.

I recently conducted a survey of almost 200 presbyters around the country on how they are attempting to make their meetings more relational. One minister from a remote area of New Mexico recognized the need for ministry wives to be in community and decided to take action. Previously, the meetings were during the day when spouses who worked, or those who were home caring for their children, were unable to attend. By moving his meetings to the evenings, attendance has increased significantly, and ministry wives are attending and forming connections with other wives.

4. **Isolated leaders are more susceptible to pride, competition and jealousy.** Our pride keeps us from reaching out to peers because we would rather not risk them seeing us as we really are. The scriptures warn spiritual leaders of this repeatedly.

In 1 Corinthians 10:11-12, Paul says this about the sad and disappointing decisions of the Israelites, *"These things happened to them as examples and were written down as warnings for us, on whom the culmination of the ages has come. So, if you think you are standing firm, be careful that you don't fall!"*

Proverbs 16:18 tells us, *"Pride goes before destruction, a haughty spirit before a fall."*

Competition, arrogance and hyper-spirituality are all ways we try to elevate and isolate ourselves from others.

5. **Isolated leaders are at a higher risk for spiritual and vocational burnout**. According to the Barna Research Group, when it comes to ministers, there is a direct correlation between the absence of friendships and a propensity towards burnout. The correlations between higher friendship satisfaction and lower overall risk for burnout and backsliding make a compelling case for the necessity of genuine friendships among pastors.[13]

Schmidt partly attributes burnout to isolated people's lack of self-care. Scripture calls it stewardship. In her clients, she notices a lack of awareness of some of their God-given needs, one of them being rest. Part of self-care is being intentional about our safe, authentic relationships with our comrades. Along that same line, when isolation sets in, leaders often don't sleep well. Sleep deprivation is highly correlated with burnout.

Stahnke reminds us that we are hardwired—created in the image of God—to be in community. Isolation is the opposite of God's plan and a trap of the enemy; it walls us off from others. The lack of friendship cuts us off from the emotional support we need to deal with the complexities of ministry life, our temptations and failures. Isolation hinders our ability to recover, ultimately leading us to burnout.

If I had to sum it up, the greatest consequence of isolation is that we end up feeling trapped. As Rusty George says in his book, *Better Together*, "The saddest truth is we are the ones who have locked the door from the inside."[14]

MAKING IT REAL: Questions for personal reflection or group discussion.

1. Gene mentioned that the enemy will exploit our weaknesses by using some form of isolation. What forms of isolation are most prevalent in ministry and how does the Devil capitalize on them?
2. Has your own circle of ministry relationships been touched by ministerial suicide? How did it effect you emotionally? What was your own take-away?
3. Jim Hawkins says that a minister's close and authentic relationships can be both a preventive medicine and an antidote for emotional wounds, mental illness, depression and even some addictions. How might a minister begin developing these kinds of friendships? Do you have them in your own life?
4. Gene's survey of over 200 sectional presbyters revealed that most ministers' meetings do not accommodate spouses. How can you help to facilitate a deeper sense of peer relationships for your spouse?
5. Has there been a time in your life when you have felt isolated?
   - What did isolation cost you emotionally during that time?
   - What has isolation cost you relationally?
   - What has isolation cost you spiritually?
6. Sometimes the cost is in our physical body. Andrew Stoeklein confessed to being "weak and tired". Do you

relate to feeling weak and tired? If so, how long would you say you have been tired? (tired for any reason)

7. Are you reluctant to risk authentic sharing with your peers? It is a risk. Have you ever tried to share transparently with a peer? How did it turn out?

Chapter 3

Epic Fails: Why We Choose Isolation

What would make us willing to gamble on the high price of isolation? The answer lies much deeper than external factors. The fact of the matter is that there are powerful forces working within us to actually choose isolation. There are a myriad of reasons for choosing to isolate ourselves, but through my research and experience, I have identified ten of the most common.

1. **Temperamental tendencies**. We are all wired differently. Some are extroverts and others are introverts; some are relational and others are more independent. Melancholy and phlegmatic personality types tend to be more shy, reserved, unsociable and hesitant. If we are not careful, we can write off the absence of community in our lives as a temperamental issue and deprive ourselves of the benefits of community.[15] We may tell ourselves, "I'm an introvert, so I don't need community," or "I'm an extrovert; I have lots of friends." We allow the excuse of our temperament to be our ticket out, rather than making an effort to seek deep, meaningful relationships.

   Our experts have some insight on early warning signs that this form of willful isolation might be playing out in the lives of pastors and their spouses. Stahnke believes there are five main signs that people may exhibit. First is a general anxiety about interacting with others. A second sign is feelings of superiority, and a notion that they don't need anyone. Third is feelings of inferiority where they think they're not good enough, no one cares, and they won't be missed. Next is simply avoiding opportunities to connect. Last is creating reasons to justify being alone.

Similarly, Schmidt looks for people's tendencies to withdraw socially. They may be less interested in participating in church or district activities, or may experience general fatigue. Ministers' wives are often tired physically, but also feel drained emotionally. She watches for feelings of being less satisfied or less excited about activities that once brought pleasure, becoming less engaging than normal, or experiencing a general dissatisfaction with life. Frequently there are physical symptoms that also arise, such as more flu, sore throats, and headaches.

Through my own personal circumstances, I have also come to understand the tendency to gravitate toward isolation. Two years ago, my wife and I lost our 23-year-old son, who was our youth pastor, to a seven-month battle with cancer. Both of us are very relational people who have always loved welcoming guests into our home, but we started feeling a draw away from people. We no longer enjoyed being in those types of settings, we began to dread evening obligations and stopped inviting people over. Recognizing this, we began making a conscious effort to push through those feelings and asked God to make us more sensitive to others. We understood that these tendencies would have taken us deeper into isolation and away from healing and community. Because of our experience, I can relate to that inward pull that is easy to give in to if we don't hold ourselves accountable to seek and maintain meaningful relationships.

2. **Criticism overload.** Many of the interactions we have involve someone wanting us to do more, be more and say more. Our activist culture of critique can become overwhelming for even the most secure ministry couple. As a result, we feel like we always need to be prepared to defend, explain or sell a decision. Criticism overload can

make us leery of relationships that might go deeper than surface level.

Schmidt and Stahnke have seen this form of isolation play out in the lives of pastors and their spouses. Schmidt observes that criticism is very stressful on the spouse as well. Disapproval can be downright discouraging and often brings to the forefront the misbelief that we have more power than we actually have. It seems to take time to learn that we have no control over how people respond to us. However, learning this is a process, and until we do, we feel more pain than we need to.

Furthermore, congregants are often immature and have not had any "tutorials" for how to register negative information without appearing hostile. What helps the most is to process this with a safe person or people. A general description of the situation to a trusted friend or colleague will suffice; no names are necessary. If we don't, we put these feelings of anger, frustration, discouragement and defeat into emotional storage—and they continue to grow. Wisdom instructs us to accept the way God made us, and resist the temptation to keep it private.

When Stahnke went into ministry 40 years ago, he was told that familiarity breeds contempt, and not to let people get too close. "Hurt me once, shame on you; hurt me twice, shame on me," was the mantra. Self-protection was the result. The pastor or spouse may talk of the importance of community and seem to be open and surrounded by people, but relationally he/she is self-protective and lonely. Keeping others at a distance feels safer, therefore no one can genuinely speak into his/her life.

3. **Lack of margin.** Contemporary ministry is a 24/7 adventure. Even though we have different compartments of our lives, the life of a minister has little margin. The dinner appointment turns into a discussion about a new ministry your guest wants to start. Our day off is interrupted by the call from someone who says, "I know this is your day off, BUT..." The church friends at your child's baseball game think it is the perfect time to monopolize your attention talking to you about church life. We live, eat, sleep and play

with the people to whom we minister. As a result, we can feel like we are always at work and forever on the clock.

When consulted about some ways to avoid this type of isolation, Schmidt again references self-care. She believes part of leaders' self-care is having a sense of personal structure to the way they do life. It's a skill that combats bombardment. This skill is developed intentionally, and frees them from feeling guilty when they sometimes tend to their own desires instead of always dropping everything for someone else. She encourages ministry spouses to prepare the sentence in advance, and be ready for that frequent name popping up on their caller ID. You know, that person who asks for five minutes but will talk for 40. Boundaries are God's idea, and they keep us from isolation and burn out trying to help others.

Stahnke also stresses the importance of being intentional. He says that community doesn't just happen. We need to make time for it by putting it on our calendars. Then, whatever is on the calendar first should not be changed unless it is an emergency. But Stahnke insists you must be the one to define an emergency. Practicing this ensures that we don't allow ourselves to be driven by the tyranny of the urgent.

4. **Pain of betrayal.** Many ministers have had their words, transparency or friendships with people in the church come back to bite them. I have had friends fired for things they said, during moments of vulnerable transparency, to someone they thought they could trust. So, instead of risking betrayal, we may avoid the risk of relationships altogether.

In her practice, Schmidt has sat with dozens of tearful ministry spouses, who are trying to process this hurt. It appears many of us have not been taught that it is our own personal responsibility to take care of ourselves when these painful events happen to us. Often, there is no substitute for a professional. She has seen an increase in ministry leaders and spouses consulting professionals, which she considers a positive step toward mental health.

Also, she points out that we don't need a lot of "safe" people in our lives. One or two trusted individuals will suffice. These people are separate from the larger group with which we share and have fellowship. Ministry injuries can fester, tempting the leader or spouse to grow a cocoon of silence, where we end up alone and vulnerable—isolated. We all need at least one person who will listen with compassion, and who respects confidentiality.

Stahnke recommends two helpful books on this subject: *Wounded by God's People* by Anne Graham Lotz, and *Safe People* by Drs. Henry Cloud and John Townsend. He stresses the need to be honest with ourselves and realize that we may have been betrayed, but we have also, at one time or another, wounded others. Forgiveness is key. The consequence of isolation will always be greater than the pain of relationship, and is worth taking the risk.

These trusting relationships may come into our lives in unexpected ways. Every one that I have developed, I did not necessarily foresee happening. This reinforces how critical it is to open up and let our guard down, in order to test the potential of relationships. I call it "test driving" friendships and although it can feel like a risk, it can lead to a big payoff in terms of finding a true confidant.

5. **Vocational transference.** Sometimes we make the mistake of confusing the "people work" of ministry with relationship. The ministry we do with people can't substitute for our own personal need for relationship and community. Mark Brouwer, in his article, *"Where Can Pastors Find Real Friends?"* states, "You just can't have a transparent peer friendship with someone who looks to you as their spiritual leader."[16]

Stahnke believes that being in "people work" alone cannot substitute for meaningful relationships because the minister is focusing on someone else's needs. This type of relationship has a tendency to feel detached and one-sided. However, friendships are intentionally focused on their collective needs, and doing life together in a more intimate and connected setting.

The powerful differential between ministers and the people they shepherd is the major sticking point for Schmidt. It prohibits truly transparent relationships and isn't good for either party, for the same reason that parents don't bring their personal issues to their children for resolution. "People work" can be quite satisfying, but it is not reciprocal. It may be sufficient for fellowship in general, but "people" are not substitutes for a trusted person who can hear and contain your heartache while promising confidentiality.

6. **Relational laziness.** Sometimes we're isolated because we prefer to be. Relationships and community are hard work and can be expensive. It requires time, energy, money, inconvenience and lots of effort. And, that doesn't even count the hidden costs.

Some of this preference for isolation, according to Schmidt, is due to not growing up in an environment where we were exposed to personal, authentic sharing. Some have incubated in a family of silence and non-disclosure. Once we are adults, we can fill in this gap and learn about this fulfilling level of communication that God intended for us to know. People who are uncomfortable with this simply haven't experienced enough of it. The body of Christ is often a healing place to learn.

Stahnke attributes much of this preference for isolation to the time factor. Ministers provide multiple services and duties, and many are bi-vocational, barely leaving time for their families. At home, kids' activities have the minister and spouse going in different directions, leaving them both exhausted with little time, energy or desire to pursue relationships.

7. **Hiding sin.** When our lives are absent of accountability, it becomes easier and easier to sin. A lack of accountability leads to sin, and then sin causes us to withdraw and hide from God and others. The third chapter of Genesis shows an example of how hiding is part of our sin nature. After Adam

and Eve sinned, they withdrew from fellowship with God and tried to hide from him.

According to Schmidt, this subject is particularly toxic because it breeds shame. Hiding is our basic tendency since the Garden, and when we do so, we cut ourselves off from love. If anyone is carrying a "secret" like that, the enemy is delighted. Often, the ministry leader doesn't know whom to confide in because of the sensitive or embarrassing nature of an event. This type of situation is a perfect example of the need for a professional. The therapist doesn't know us as "Pastor Johnson" and doesn't hear our story as incriminating. Trained professionals hear our stories as personal experiences that still need to be processed and worked through.

Confessing is healthy, since carrying a burden of secrecy has consequences of its own, in terms of mental and physical health. As leaders become more comfortable with "confessing our faults" it begins to lose its stigma. A common theme among ministry spouses is never having had a place to process former church hurts. Some of these are traumatic, like being voted out of a congregation, for example. Telling our stories to a safe person brings relief.

Stahnke states that sin itself leads to hiding and isolation. It's a "fear of loss" response—loss of reputation, prestige, income, position or relationships with others. This type of isolation leads to the loss of mercy, grace and healing of the soul. Instead of prospering, we live lives of desperation, filled with guilt and shame. It's better to self-disclose and allow the grace of God to work in our lives than to be exposed and deal with the fallout. If we are proactive in confessing our sin, we aren't forced to be reactive, or have others be reactive toward us. He identifies a few verses from scripture that address this topic:

- *"Be sure your sin will find you out."* (Numbers 32:23, Joshua 22:1)

- *"Whoever conceals his transgressions will not prosper, but he who confesses and forsakes them will obtain mercy."* (Proverbs 28:13 ESV)
- *"Confess to one another therefore your faults [your slips, your false steps, your offenses, your sins] and pray (also) for one another, that you may be healed and restored [to a spiritual tone of mind and heart]. The earnest [heartfelt, continued] prayer of a righteous man makes tremendous power available [dynamic in its working]."* (James 5:16 AMPC)

8. **Unstable success.** Success can pull us into an endless maze of our own achievement. We can end up living in a make-believe world of self. A real-life illustration of this tendency was the suicide of mega church pastor, Andrew Stoecklein, that we referenced earlier. He had a thriving church, wonderful family, supportive parents and mentors, and seemingly everything but the ability and foundation to shoulder the strong emotions that come with ministry. And, unfortunately for him and his family, it ended tragically.

Stahnke has identified some warning signs that our own pride and successes may be isolating us. They include:
- Laziness in spiritual disciplines
- Disregard for the Scripture
- Resistance to, or resentment toward, meaningful accountability
- Becoming conceited or arrogant; having a sense of superiority
- Narcissism, or a sense of entitlement

In Schmidt's experience, when the success of ministry becomes too important, family relationships begin to suffer. More specifically, the spouse may feel the decreasing availability of his/her companion. Having to cancel or cut short a vacation, missing a child's games and performances because of board meetings or other church commitments, or not adhering to date nights may all indicate ministry success. But, ominously, the decline in the health of our homes and marriages is taking a hit and requires healing.

For young ministers, this can be one of the most counterintuitive ideas because we are constantly putting our all into building stability, building a successful ministry and building good leaders we can rely upon. It's difficult to make a conscious choice about self-care and carving out time for our families. But, if our families aren't there, it doesn't matter what successes we have in the church building or what relationships we build in the city. If we don't pay attention to those critical things, we'll fail.

9. **Emotional disorders.** Henry Cloud's and John Townsend's book, *Safe People*, contains a wonderful chapter entitled, "Why Do I Isolate Myself From People?"[17] where they address the dynamics of withdrawal and isolation. They explain how emotional disorders like broken-heartedness, abandonment, attachment, emotional abuse, perfectionism, fake sense of self-sufficiency, and even passivity can contribute to painful isolation, and even worse consequences.

Schmidt also recommends *Safe People* for those who want to learn how to overcome past pain and identify healthy friends. She states that no one is born with an emotional disorder. When one occurs, it's likely that there has been a string of events dating back a couple of decades, from which the person did not fully recover at the time. It is rarely a single event. To employ a figure of speech, it's the "haystack," not the "last straw" that's the problem. Staying connected with safe people and not isolating ourselves is a form of "haystack reduction." Eventually, years of anxiety and worry can morph into panic attacks or even post-traumatic stress disorder. Years of feeling unnecessary, invisible, tired, frustrated, neglected and overworked can collapse into clinical depression.

Schmidt reminds us that these conditions are highly treatable. One of her mentors, Dr. Richard Dobbins of Emerge Ministries, used to say to his students: "In therapy, we can make very few things perfect. But there are very few things that can't be made significantly better."

In Stahnke's practice, he sees emotional disorders like depression, social anxiety, various addictions and abusive behavior resulting from withdrawal and isolation.

10. **Epidemic of self.** We have become a pretty narcissistic culture that is selling "me" at the expense of "us." We don't have to look too far to find it.
   - Selfies have replaced group photos
   - Self-branding has replaced group identity
   - Me is more appealing than us
   - Control trumps collaboration
   - DIY (do it yourself) has replaced DIT (do it together)
   - Parents don't take their kids to youth services, but want them to feel included in the group they have isolated themselves from
   - People's expectations far exceed their commitment level
   - Facebook posts advertise parts of our lives that were once discreetly private

Although these seem like a random collection of trends, they all are rooted in narcissism and an infatuation with self. The article, *Me, Me, Me! America's Narcissism Epidemic,* states that, "The United States is currently suffering from an epidemic of narcissism. Narcissism both clinically and personally is accelerating faster each decade."[18]

Narcissism infiltrated the pew decades ago, but now it has finally caught root in the philosophy and leadership style of pastors. When deciding whether to return emails and phone calls, attend district events, spend time and build relationships with people whose ministry is smaller than ours, pastors seem to be filtering every opportunity through the question, "What's in it for me?" That kind of philosophy never takes us to community. It only robs us of the relationships we hope to find and leaves us stranded on the island of self.

Maybe the Holy Spirit convicted you about one of these toxic choices in your own life. All ten of these factors make us feel like no one listens, no one understands us and that we are all alone. That is a lie from the Devil. The truth is we need real, intimate, vulnerable friendships if we are going to last in ministry.

MAKING IT REAL: Questions for personal reflection or group discussion.

1. Gene begins this chapter by saying that isolation is often a choice. Do you agree with this? Why or why not?
2. Counselor Susan Schmidt said she is seeing an increase in the number of ministers who consult with a professional counselor in trying to process emotional wounds. Although she and George Stahnke believe this is good, many ministers have a stigma about seeking the help of counselors. Why do you think this is? What can a professional provide that others may not be able to?
3. Do you see your temperament or family background contributing to isolation in your life?
4. This chapter identifies ten of the most common reasons we choose to be isolated. They are:
   - Temperamental tendencies. We use our temperament as an excuse.
   - Criticism overload. Criticism makes us leery of people and relationships.
   - Lack of margin. Our lives lack the time that relationships require.
   - Pain of betrayal. We avoid relationships fearing betrayal.
   - Vocational transference. We mistake "people work" for relationships.
   - Relational laziness. We don't want to give what relationships require.
   - Secret sin. We avoid relationships to better hide sin in our lives.

- Unstable success. We are promoted above our maturity.
- Emotional disorders. We are hindered by unresolved pain and disappointment from the past.
- Narcissism. We become self-absorbed and self-centered.

Discuss how each one might manifest itself in ministry. Then have each person be transparent in identifying three that the enemy might capitalize upon in their own life.

5. Pray with and for one another regarding the list above.

Chapter 4

Spiritual DNA: Why We Need Community

The bottom line is we all need community. The need for relationships goes back to the creation of Eve for Adam, and was reinforced in the New Testament in Paul's letters to the early Church. Even he was not too spiritual or proud to discount community, writing:

> *"I long to see you so that I may impart to you some spiritual gift to make you strong—that is, that you and I may be mutually encouraged by each other's faith." Romans 1:11-12*

Aside from being an innate desire since creation, community helps make our lives rich and full, keeps us accountable, helps us discover and remedy our flaws, and has numerous other benefits. I think it's beneficial to mention a few specific reasons why we need community, and why it is worth pursuing.

1. **Design**. Community is part of our divine design. However, it's important to note that community started with the Trinity long before creation. Notice that in the creation account, God used plural pronouns in Genesis 1:16 to refer to Himself saying, *"Let **US** make mankind in **OUR** image, in **OUR** likeness."* Then after creating Adam, God said, *"It is not good for man to be alone." (Genesis 2:18)*

To illustrate this, I like to use the analogy of blowing up a balloon. When I blow it up, air is not the only thing that enters. Tiny droplets of saliva are blown into the balloon, and that saliva has pieces of my DNA. A DNA lab could get my DNA from that balloon without ever taking blood or swabbing my mouth. When God breathed His image and life into humanity, we got a piece of Him. Part of that "image" or "Spiritual DNA," as I like to call it, is a need for community.

But not only was community modeled in the Trinity and prescribed for humanity at creation, it was the prayerful hope of Jesus when he prayed for us. Two times in John 17 Jesus prayed that our sense of community would reflect the community that exists between Him and the Father. Jesus prayed in John 17:11, *"Father, protect them so that they may be one as we are one,"* and again in verse 21, *"My prayer is...that all of them may be one, Father, just as you are in me and I am in you."* God doesn't live in isolation and he did not create us to either.

When I asked Phil Steiger, from Every Thought Captive, about the theological ramifications of this truth, he pointed out that in the beginning, God created us male and female, in His image. Two of our first hints as to what that means is the implication that God is more than one—the Triune Elohim—and then the need for Adam to have an appropriate companion. Creation in all of its splendor was not the right companion for the first human. Only the second human (Eve) could meet that standard. Then, those two were given the mandate to fill the earth with even more like them.

The assumption that we were created to flourish together doesn't stop there. Much of the Old Testament is full of instruction on how people are to live in cities and thrive together as a community. Many of the "you" pronouns in Paul's letters are plural. They literally refer to the church as a whole, not just individuals. The next time you read Paul wishes "you" grace and peace, imagine the church. Imagine yourself in a pew next to a brother or sister in Christ worshiping your God and reading His Word together, instead of imagining yourself alone with your Bible and journal.

We are fish that swim in individualistic waters. I read the Bible with the assumption that I am in view when Scripture talks about discipleship. And, while I clearly need to grow in Christ-likeness, so do we. I need *you* in order to draw closer to Christ, and you also need *me* to do the same, so that together we can walk side by side on our way to God.

I have learned that one of the antidotes to the pain that comes with broken or dysfunctional community is friendship—it's not less community, but better community. Pastoring isn't for wimps, and one of the things that makes it hard are the relational strains we go through. People we pour our lives (and sometimes money) into often turn on us, tell us how bad we are at taking care of people, and then leave for the church on the other side of town—or no church at all. There is no getting around it; that hurts.

As a result, a temptation we face is to close ourselves up—to avoid the kinds of relationships that will cause that kind of pain in the future. We can resist that temptation by cultivating and holding onto healthy friendships. I have learned to touch base with strong friends when I am reeling from a strained or severed relationship.

But that makes perfect, biblical sense. We were literally created to flourish inside sound communities: being married to our best friend, family members we love grilling for, friends who remember you when you rocked a mullet, friends who will be there when you lose your job. It's how God intended it.[19]

2. **Congruency**. If we were made for relationship, then we are most incongruent, inconsistent and unnatural when we exist in isolation. When we deprive ourselves of relationships, we can't function as the people God created us to be. I think that's what God meant when he said, *"It is not good for man to be alone." (Genesis 2:18)*

Paul taught that being part of Christ is inseparable from being a member of the community of faith. Paul said, *"Just as a body, though one, has many parts, but all its many parts form one body, so it is with Christ." (1 Corinthians 12:12)*

By this, we know that relationships are the channel God uses to grow and mature us into the people He wants us to be.

3. **Enrichment.** Your soul is refreshed when you serve, partner and build relationships with other leaders. As I mentioned earlier, in an interview with Barna Research, family therapist and former pastor, Jim Hawkins, contends that close, authentic relationships are both preventive medicine and a restorative antidote for a host of emotional wounds and mental illness, including depression and addiction.[20] Hawkins says,

> "Our minds and emotions are healthiest when we maintain strong attachments to people with whom we can be open, honest and vulnerable."[21]

> Paul spoke of this when he said, *"I was glad when Stephanas, Fortunatus and Achaicus arrived ... For they refreshed my spirit and yours also." (1 Corinthians 16:17,18)* The Proverbs also affirm the value of relationships saying, *"As iron sharpens iron, so one person sharpens another." (Proverbs 27:17)* We are our best selves when we're in community. We are our worst selves when we live in isolation.

4. **Accountability**. Relationships give us staying power. They enrich our lives, affirm our purpose, provide accountability, compensate for our weaknesses and anchor us in community. In his book, *Survive or Thrive*, Jimmy Dodd uses the Johari Window to illustrate the importance of relationships in our personal growth.[22] Imagine a four-pane window with two windows stacked on top of each other.

JOHARI WINDOW		
	WHAT I KNOW ABOUT ME	WHAT I DON'T KNOW ABOUT ME
WHAT YOU KNOW ABOUT ME	OPEN / PUBLIC	BLIND SPOT
WHAT YOU DON'T KNOW ABOUT ME	PRIVATE / SECRET	HIDDEN

This version of the Johari grid reveals four areas.

- First, if I and my friends know something about me and it is known to both of us it is open and public (top left).
- Second, if I know something about myself that my friends don't know, it is private or in some cases a secret (bottom left).
- Third, if some information about me is not known or realized by me nor my friends, it is hidden (bottom right).
- Fourth, if something about me is unknown to myself, but known to my friends, it is a blind spot (upper right).

This means there are three areas of my life that friends can help (open/public, private/secret and blind spots). One of those is our blind spots (upper right) that makes relationships extremely important. Our friends can help us see weaknesses we are blind to, but are obvious to others. A scriptural example of this is in 2 Samuel 12:1-15, where God confronts David about a blind spot through a trusted friend and prophet, Nathan. In addition, there is a fourth area that is unknown to both me and my friends, and only accessible through the Holy Spirit convicting, leading and revealing to us or Spirit-driven friends.

5. **Belonging**. Relationships are what gives us a sense of belonging, fulfillment and hope. They are the context from which we find meaning and discover the lasting contributions we can make in the lives of others. Paul employed the analogy of body parts being unable to deny their need for each other to communicate our own need for community saying, *"The eye cannot say to the hand, 'I don't need you!'"* (1 Corinthians 12:21-27)

6. **Effectiveness.** Jesus could have embraced many different styles of leadership, but he chose to model and lead through

relationships and community. He selected a team of twelve disciples (Matthew 10:1-4), commissioned 36 small teams for evangelism (Luke 10:1), and formed a strong "inner circle" as confidants and a personal support group (Mark 5:37, Mark 9:2, Mark 14:32-35). Those leaders, minus one, successfully launched the entire movement of Christianity. This community and team model is the best one for all of us to follow.

The Lilly Endowment invested $84 million over 10 years to study what enabled Christian pastors in America to sustain excellence over many years. They funded 63 projects across 25 different denominations and traditions. Each organization made a similar discovery—relationships with peers is the key factor to pastoral longevity.[23]

7. **Collaboration.** Throughout the Bible and human history, God has used collaborative relationships to create organizations and build His Kingdom. Relationships are the life-blood that give those structures vitality, energy and a sense of community. When we fail to be relational, the organizations we serve, be it a church or a district, are starved of their power and deprived of their highest potential. It's an organizational death wish!

8. **Longevity.** Proverbs 17:17 says, *"A friend loves at all times, and a brother is born for a difficult time."* Statistics show that few things bring excellence and longevity to your ministry more than peer relationships. To reiterate a point from the previous page, The Lilly Endowment study deemed peer relationships the most important factor in pastoral longevity.[24]

The need for longevity can't be overstated. Richard Clinton, professor of leadership at Fuller Theological Seminary, has studied the legacy of biblical leaders. He makes a poignant observation that few finished well. There are around 800 leaders mentioned in the Bible. Of those 800, 100 of them have enough data to be able to interpret their leadership. About 50 of these have enough data to evaluate their finish. About one in three finished well. Modern statistics indicate that this ratio is probably generous. Nearly 70% of today's pastors will not retire from the ministry. In other words, Clinton believes that less than one in three will "finish well."[25]

9. **Authenticity**. If we claim relationships are important for the people we lead, then we must model that priority in our own lives. If we don't there will always be something about us that is artificial.

MAKING IT REAL: Questions for personal reflection or group discussion.

1. When you think back upon the healthiest seasons of your life, do you also find the existence of healthy relationships? Who were those people and what did they deposit into your life?
2. What obstacles would or did you have to overcome to develop peer level relationships?
3. How have you cultivated and maintained peer level relationships?
4. Can you give a specific example of how peer relationships have helped you through a difficult time? Briefly explain.
5. When your peer chooses to share openly and honestly with you privately, do you feel insecure about how you should respond? Do you hesitate because you think you might make it worse?
6. As a ministry wife, do you feel a desire to connect with other ministry wives? What thoughts do you have about connecting with other ministry wives in an organized fashion similar to what the men are doing?
7. Gene talked about nine reasons we all need community. They were:
   - Design. God designed us for community.
   - Congruency. We are our best selves when we exist in community.

- Enrichment. Life is richer when we exist in community.
- Accountability. Community compensates for our blind spots and weaknesses.
- Belonging. Community gives us a sense of belonging.
- Effectiveness. We are more effective when we function inside of community.
- Collaboration. God uses community to build His Kingdom.
- Longevity. We have more perseverance and grit in community.
- Authenticity. We are more authentic when we model the community we tell others to seek.

Have each person identify and share three that they most need and value on a personal level.

Chapter 5

Jail Break: Escaping Isolation

Once you've established a pattern of isolation in your life, it's critical to take steps to break its spell over you and rediscover community. We need to intentionally refocus on what community is. Looking at the word in a spiritual context, I would describe it as "a feeling of belonging with others, as a result of sharing common attitudes, interests, goals and spiritual priorities." If you find yourself moving away from community, there are six practical ways to break free from isolation.

1. **Take the initiative.** I don't think I've ever met a pastor who doesn't believe in community. We preach and teach on it. We tell people that's why they need consistency in church attendance and to be part of a small group. Everyone believes in community. The problem is, as Joe Battaglia says in his book, *Unfriended*, "Community just does not work without commune."[26] The commune part of the word is the one we struggle with. Why? Commune takes time, can't be delegated and has delayed rewards.

    But no friendship, district budget, nor any amount of inclusion can trump the absence of our will to work toward community. We have to take responsibility for making an effort. In Galatians chapter 6, Paul teaches us to *"bear the burdens"* of others, in the sense of sympathizing with others in their troubles. But then, in verse five he says, *"Each man must carry his own load." (Galatians 6:5)* In other words, at the end of the day, each one of us must take responsibility to initiate relationships, contribute to community and step outside our own comfort zones. Most of the time we're living on islands because we choose to.

2. **Connect with a network you don't lead.** Community is like a retirement account. It takes trial and error and isn't built overnight. We have to be willing to "test drive" relationships to see which ones click. The easiest way to accomplish this is to connect with existing networks. These networks might be your sectional meetings, social gatherings in your district, or even District Council. When you need a new cell phone, you don't look for them in elevators—you go to a cell phone store! If you need relationships, you need to hang out where those are most likely to happen.

3. **Apply the "Three Friend Principle."** The three friend principle has many different applications, but basically indicates we always need three different people in our lives to fulfill three critical roles (accountability, friendship and mentoring).

In Craig Groeschel's book, *Divine Direction*, the chapter entitled, "Connect," states,

"Consider the three types of friends everyone needs to reach their God-given potential: (1) a **friend to challenge** you and bring out your best, (2) a **friend to help you find strength in God and to grow in your faith**, and (3) **a friend to tell you the truth**, especially when you don't want to hear it."[27]

The book, *Safe People*, that I mentioned previously, identifies another model claiming we all need three kinds of people in our lives.[28] We need (1) a friend who draws us closer to God, (2) a friend who draws us closer to others, and (3) a friend who helps us become all that God created us to be.

My favorite three friend application is called the "PTB Model."[29] It identifies three key relationships every pastor needs: (1) a **P**aul (a mentor), (2) a **T**imothy (someone to disciple), and (3) a **B**arnabas (a peer to encourage and be encouraged by).

Employing any of these models will ensure that we have those three critical people in our lives, so choose whichever one resonates most with you personally.

4. **Develop "real time" peer relationships.** I've found the people best suited to be a pastor's friend are fellow pastors, most often those in a different church. Notice I did not say a Facebook group, Twitter or some other social media application. Those do serve a purpose, but the more time we invest in an artificial community, the more we become artificial. We need face-to-face real time interaction. I am more likely to get to know, appreciate and learn from people I spend time with face-to-face. It's when we spend time together that I learn your passions, joys, sorrows, calling and friendship. Some call it "real time," I call it "face-to-face," and author Joe Battaglia calls it "intersecting in real space."[30]

Our professionals weighed in on this subject, with Schmidt noting that peers bring a wealth of common ground. The key is that peers have a similar calling as a shepherd, a similar desire to know God, a similar love of the sheep, and similar knowledge of the business demands of the church. Our peers have walked in our shoes and shouldered the burdens we bear. They can speak into our lives with credibility and sincere care. Then, we can reciprocate by offering the same to them. Peers can bring a time-worn humility; they share a common concern about ministry stresses on the family. Peers help us develop endurance reserves. It's critically important to find a peer, and then be a peer.

Similarly, Stahnke reiterates that in peer-level relationships, we share common goals, challenges, and values. In essence, we speak the same language. We can relate to one another with greater ease and empathy.

There are a few very good reasons why peer relationships with ministers outside our church make sense.

- **Commonality**. Other pastors are people who can immediately relate to our situation. They have similar jobs, calling, struggles, family dynamics and seasons of life.
- **Momentum**. Because we already have so much in common, even a new friendship has instant traction and does not require months or years of initial investment.
- **Safe**. Because they are not part of our staff or church, we can confide in them without losing confidence or credibility within our own local context.
- **Empathy**. They are already familiar with the kind of struggles, obstacles and support we need.
- **Availability**. They have similar work schedules and are more likely to share the same seasons, days and hours of availability.
- **Energizing**. Friendships with those outside of our ministry context allows our relationships to breathe air that is refreshing and unrelated to the normal culture and vibe of our churches.
- **Prayer support**. We can ask for prayer from a peer without worrying about losing respect, confidence or credibility from lay leaders in our church.

In Romans 16, Paul closes the book by greeting a long list of ministry friends that he describes as "coworkers." Paul knew that life was too short and ministry was too hard to do it alone. He didn't just write letters to people. He got in the trenches of relationships with other ministers and colleagues. We should, too.

5. **Get a life outside of ministry.** Take the initiative to build a sense of community outside of our ministry context. Find:

- Common **interests** (sports, camping, hunting, running, hiking or reading)
- Common **seasons of life** (single, young married, young families, parents of teens, empty nesters, retired)
- Common **ministry settings** (rural, urban, suburban)

However, we cannot limit ourselves only to commonalities. Sometimes the best friendships are waiting for us outside our comfort zone. Today, I love wilderness camping. It wasn't always that way. I had been a camper for many years, but it was when I found a new relationship with my friend, George Stahnke, that my fondness for him caused me to learn it as well, so we could camp together.

6. **Get periodic emotional check-ups.** Because God created us for community, the sin nature in each of us will seek to express itself in some form of isolation. It will be different for each of us. For some, it may be broken-heartedness, abandonment, attachment or emotional abuse. For others, it may be competition, jealousy, perfectionism, self-sufficiency or even extreme passivity. Each one of us must answer to God for our own actions, take responsibility for our own individual problems, and grow.

The important thing is to make one of our strengths that we know our weaknesses. One of the ways we can do this is to acknowledge the difficult nature of modern ministry and take responsibility for our own emotional health. That's why I believe checking in with a Christian counselor at least every five years is a must. There are wonderful Christian people who are gifted, trained and skilled at helping us see weaknesses and helping us fight our own demons. Mark Brouwer wrote a great article in *Christianity Today* about the importance of pastors understanding ourselves and what is contributing to our isolation.[31]

Also, modern ministry is so much more demanding and taxing upon our bodies, souls and spirits than it was 20 years ago. Getting an "emotional check-up" from a licensed therapist every few years has personally helped keep me accountable and build a firewall around my mind, my marriage and my family life.

The sticking point for many may be the unknown regarding what type of professional to seek, how many sessions might it take, what topics would be covered, what to expect during a session, and what the cost might be. Our professionals discussed each of these items, and some of the tools they use in their own practices

For Schmidt, she takes a history to learn her client's back story, even from before he/she went into ministry. As a basic screening, she uses the Beck Depression Inventory or Beck Anxiety Inventory, which is very quick to take, and to score, right in the office. She gets the most valuable information from her clients by hearing them tell her their story in their own words; by finding out what has transpired since they last met. She goes by what she observes in front of her when deciding the next step to take.

She also feels strongly about having a check-up with a medical doctor, since physical concerns always need to come before emotional or spiritual issues. Some health conditions, such as low thyroid, can actually mimic the symptoms of depression or anxiety. Lack of sleep can also play into emotional health.

Schmidt observes that the cost of counseling varies geographically across the nation, and according to what kind of a counselor or therapist a person chooses. There are a variety of choices, including licensed professional counselors, marriage and family therapists, psychologists or psychiatrists. There are certain services a counselor is not able to provide, such as prescription medications, making a referral to your family doctor in those cases. Ideally, a person could expect a counseling appointment to cost about $120 per session on the West Coast. But, she highly encourages getting the spouse involved in the counseling as well, which would add to the cost.

From Stahnke's perspective, he believes it would take between two and four sessions to go through specific inventories, depending on the individual need and situation of the client. His estimated cost is around $80 per one-hour session. He recommends the following topics and inventories being addressed or completed:[32]

- Heart Inventory—Identifying your reactive cycle: http://www.renewalcs.org/wp-content/uploads/2016/06/Heart-Inventory.pdf
- Marriage Stability Quiz: http://www.renewalcs.org/wp-content/uploads/2016/06/marriage_stability_test.pdf
- Assessment of Marital Purity: http://www.renewalcs.org/wp-content/uploads/2016/05/purityassessment.pdf
- Stress and Burnout Inventory
- Hamilton Survey for Emotional and Physical Health: http://www.renewalcs.org/wp-content/uploads/2016/06/hamilton_survey_for_emotional_and_physical_wellness.pdf

As helpful as these five things are, nothing and I mean nothing can take the place of you tying practical actions to good intentions. We can only feel part of what we are connected to. So, what one thing can you do today to take a step in the right direction? Anything else is a step away from goodness.

MAKING IT REAL: Questions for personal reflection or group discussion.

1. What are practical ways individuals can take the initiative in building a deeper sense of community among the ministers in their area or region?
2. How might your section, region or district structure meetings and events to build a greater sense of community?
3. Gene talked about the three friend principle, that every person should have three people in their life.
   - Someone to be accountable to

- Someone to have a genuine friendship with
- Someone to mentor us

Which is the hardest to find and why? How might we better find this person?

4. Gene defined "real time" peer relationships as face to face interactions with fellow ministers. Why can't social media, Facebook groups or blogs substitute for this kind of interaction?

5. Pastors often make the mistake of thinking that the only valuable peer relationships are those with the same size or larger ministry than ours. Why is this philosophy dangerous and limiting?

6. What are your own thoughts about Gene's statement that modern ministry is so demanding it is worth getting an "emotional check up" with a counselor every five years?

7. Breaking out may demand a change in the way you view professional help and appropriate medications. In your world, do you see the stigma surrounding this subject to be getting better, worse, or about the same?

8. What do you get distracted by when it comes to making time to effectively engage with others?

9. How has this e-book been helpful to you?

Conclusion

Creating awareness of isolation in ministry, and the toll it takes on church leaders, is the first step in combating this pervasive issue. If you gravitate toward isolation, you are not alone. The overall take-away is that community and peer friendships are not a luxury; they are a necessity. God has designed us to lean on each other in times of need. Our ministries, families, marriages, mental health and even our very lives depend on our intentional efforts to create meaningful connections. The importance of establishing safe, trusting, vulnerable relationships with at least one or two confidants can help us process hurts and make decisions when times get especially tough. These "safe people" should be outside of the particular church family that we serve, so that we can feel free to be honest and transparent with them.

At times, consulting a professional counselor or therapist is the best way to work through issues we face in ministry, or even to resolve past hurts that occurred well before we accepted that role. Even if we feel we are not dealing with anything especially monumental, checking in with a counselor at least every few years is helpful for maintaining accountability, managing stress and protecting mental health.

Creating margin, or carving out time for ourselves, our spouses and families is not selfish. Both our mental and physical health can suffer if we allow even well-meaning church members or outside commitments to monopolize our time and our calendars. If our ministry flourishes, but we end up with nobody beside us to share in that success, we have not really succeeded at all.

About the Author

Gene Roncone has served as Lead Pastor of Highpoint Church since October 2002. Highpoint is a network of Christian ministries throughout the city of Aurora. The ministry group consists of Highpoint@Southlands, Highpoint@Colfax, Highpoint Food Group, and the Highpoint Podcast Network. In addition to pastoring, Gene serves as an Executive Presbyter for the Rocky Mountain Ministry Network and hosts two podcasts: THE COMMUNITY, a podcast for pastors on Colorado's Eastern Slope, and another called THE EXCHANGE for regional leaders in his denomination.

Gene graduated from Bethany University and then studied communications at Western Seminary and organizational development at the University of San Francisco. He has authored three books entitled *Explore the Call, Prevailing Over Impossibility* and *A Season for Legacy*. Gene enjoys reading, camping and spending time with his wife, Rhonda, and their adult children and grandchildren.

Gene can be contacted at gene@agspe.org.

Endnotes & References

Chapter 1 — Is Isolation in Ministry Real?

[1] Clinton, Richard. *Starting Well: Building a Strong Foundation for a Lifetime of Ministry*. Altadena, CA: Barnabas Publishers, 1994. 11-13.

[2] The "Isolation in Ministry" content began as a research project for a five-part PODumentary that was syndicated on two of Gene Roncone's podcasts. If you would like to listen to them in audio format click the hyperlinks below.

Part 1 – Is Isolation in Ministry Real? - www.agspe.org/3a.mp3
Part 2 – Lonely Losers: The Cost of Isolation - www.agspe.org/3b.mp3
Part 3 – Epic Fails: Why We Choose Isolation - www.agspe.org/3c.mp3
Part 4 – Why We Need Community - www.agspe.org/3d.mp3
Part 5 – Jail Break: Escaping Isolation - www.agspe.org/3e.mp3
E-BOOK: "Isolation in Ministry"- www.agspe.org/isolation.pdf

[3] Smietana, Bob. "Mental Illness Remains Taboo Topic for Many Pastors." LifeWay Research. September 22, 2014. Accessed October 17, 2018. https://lifewayresearch.com/2014/09/22/mental-illness-remains-taboo-topic-for-many-pastors.

[4] Metaxas, Eric and Roberto Rivera. "A Pastor's Suicide: An All-Too Familiar Story." The Christian Post. September 19,. 2018. Accessed October 17, 2018. https://www.christianpost.com/voice/a-pastors-suicide-an-all-too-familiar-story.html.

[5] Geiger, Eric. *How to Ruin Your Life: and Starting Over When You Do*. Nashville, TN: B&H Publishing, 2018.

[6] Barna Research Group. *The State of Pastors: How Today's Faith Leaders Are Navigating Life and Leadership in an Age of Complexity*. Ventura, CA: Barna Research, 2017. 39.

[7] LifeWay Research. Protestant Pastors Views on Ministry: Survey of 1,000 Protestant Pastors. Research Study. Nashville, TN: LifeWay Research, 2011. 6,8-9.

[8] Stahnke, George. Counselor at Focus on the Family and Renewal Ministries, Colorado Springs, CO. Personal Interview. Contact at george@renewalcs.org.

[9] Schmidt, Susan. Licensed Professional Counselor, Roseville, CA. Personal Interview. Contact at susanvschmidt@msn.com.

Chapter 2 — Lonely Losers: The Cost of Isolation

[10] Geiger, Eric. "3 Reasons Why Ministry Leaders Choose to Be Isolated." Eric Geiger. February 22, 2017. Accessed October 12, 2018. https://ericgeiger.com/2017/02/3-reasons-why-ministry-leaders-choose-to-be-isolated/.

[11] Geiger, Eric. "Isolated Leaders Are Dangerous Leaders." ChurchLeaders. May 31, 2017. Accessed October 12, 2018. https://churchleaders.com/pastors/pastor-articles/304328-isolated-leaders-are-dangerous-leaders-eric-geiger.html.

[12] Barna Research Group, 39.

[13] Ibid, 40-41.

[14] George, Rusty. *Better Together: Discover the Power of Community*. Bloomington, MN: Bethany House Publishers, 2018. 41.

Chapter 3 — Epic Fails: Why We Choose Isolation

[15] Reiland, Dan. "Why You Cannot Lead From Isolation." Ministry Today Magazine. August 25, 2016. Accessed October 14, 2018. https://ministrytodaymag.com/leadership/23109-why-you-cannot-lead-from-isolation.

[16] Brouwer, Mark. "Where Can Pastors Find Real Friends?" Christianity Today. March 2014. Accessed on October 12, 2018. https://www.christianitytoday.com/pastors/2014/march-online-only/friendless-pastor.html.

[17] Cloud, Henry and John Townsend. *Safe People: How to Find Relationships That Are Good for You and Avoid Those That Aren't*. Grand Rapids, MI: Zondervan Publishing, 1995. 123-139.

[18] Today Show. "Me, Me, Me! America's Narcissism Epidemic." Today. October 16, 2016. Accessed October 23, 2018. https://www.today.com/popculture/me-me-me-americas-narcissism-epidemic-2D80555351.
Contains excerpts from: Twenge, Jean M. and W. Keith Campbell. *The Narcissism Epidemic: Living in the Age of Entitlement*. New York: Atria Paperback, 2009.

Chapter 4 — Spiritual DNA: Why We Need Community

[19] Steiger, Phil. Lead Pastor at Living Hope Church, Colorado Springs, Colorado, and co-director of Every Thought Captive, blog and conference provider. Personal Interview. Blog at https://philsteiger.com. Contact at phil@lhcco.org.

[20] Barna Research Group, 39.

[21] Ibid, 51.

[22] Dodd, Jimmy. *Survive or Thrive: Six Relationships Every Pastor Needs*. Colorado Springs, CO: David C. Cook, 2015. 258-259.

[23] Gruden, Elliott. "Pastors Need Friends Too." Desiring God. February 10, 2018. Accessed October 12, 2018. https://www.desiringgod.org/articles/pastors-need-friends-too.

[24] Ibid

[25] Clinton, 11-13.

Chapter 5 — Jail Break: Escaping Isolation

[26] Battaglia, Joe. *Unfriended: Finding True Community in a Disconnected Culture*. Savage, MN: BroadStreet Publishing, 2018. 14.

[27] Groeschel, Craig. Chap. 6 in *Divine Direction: 7 Decisions That Will Change Your Life*. Grand Rapids, MI: Zondervan, 2017.

[28] Cloud and Townsend, 143.

[29] Barringer, Dave. "4 Ways to Escape the Pastor Isolation Trap." OutreachMagazine.com. June 13, 2017. Accessed October 14, 2018. https://outreachmagazine.com/features/23010-pastor-isolation.html.

[30] Battaglia, 50.

[31] Brouwer.

[32] The topics and inventories mentioned and recommended by Geroge Stahnke for an "emotional check-up" are listed below:
- Heart Inventory--Identifying your reactive cycle: http://www.renewalcs.org/wp-content/uploads/2016/06/Heart-Inventory.pdf
- Marriage stability quiz: http://www.renewalcs.org/wp-content/uploads/2016/06/marriage_stability_test.pdf
- Assessment of marital purity: http://www.renewalcs.org/wp-content/uploads/2016/05/purityassessment.pdf
- Stress and Burnout inventory
- Hamilton Survey for emotional and physical health: http://www.renewalcs.org/wp-content/uploads/2016/06/hamilton_survey_for_emotional_and_physical_wellness.pdf

Made in the USA
Columbia, SC
24 June 2019